# Famous Dog Quotes

By

Rodney A Drury

# Copyright © 2017 by Rodney A Drury

ISBN-13: 978-1942421139

Redneck Mystic Media
3011 N. Delaware ST.
Peoria IL 61603

# Contents

Seeing Eye to Eye ...........................................1

Food and Water ...........................................11

Relationships ...........................................17

Questions ...........................................23

Body Parts ...........................................31

Behavior ...........................................35

Poop and Pee ...........................................45

# Seeing Eye to Eye

***I'm not staring.***
– Wellington, a German Shepherd Terrier
mix

*I forgive you.*
-Ziggy, a Pekingese Poodle mix




*Babies are a lot like new born puppies.*
*Puppies are just cuter.*
-Abby, a Beagle




*If you're really sorry, you would rub my*
*belly.*
-Gatsby, a Springer Spaniel

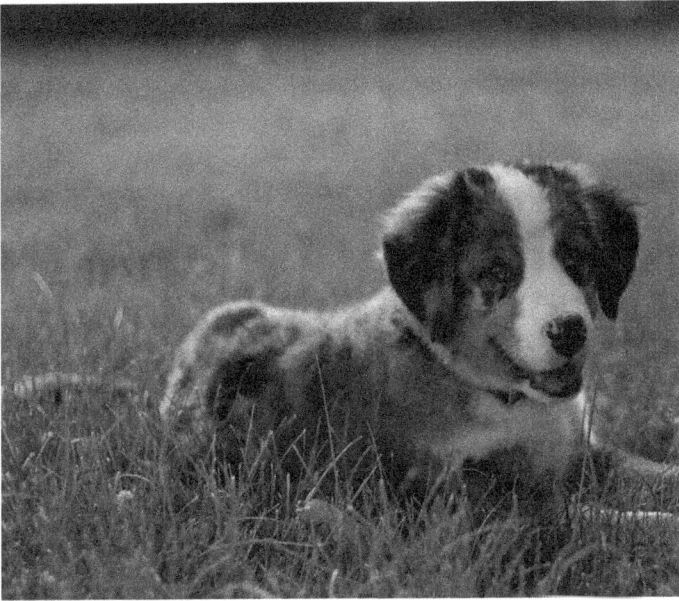

*I sleep so much because being your friend is exhausting.*
- Classy, a Yorkshire Terrier

*I'm not nagging; you're just not Listening.*
-  Veto, a Boxer


*I didn't get that because you need the exercise
more than me.*
-Hooch, a Dalmatian Retriever mix


*Shame is not just a human emotion.*
-Homer, a Collie Lab mix

***You irritate me sometimes.***
-Yoda, mixed bread

*Cats and squirrels are to the same thing.*
-Brewsky, a rescue dog


*So I'm needy, isn't everyone?*
-Zac, a mixed breed


*I only lie down in the flower bed to smell better.*
-Crash, a Great Dane

*Google it. Digging is a legitimate addiction.*
- Lazarus, an Alaskan Malamute

*What do you mean I have anger issues?*
-Rio, a Boston Terrier


*I am listening!*
-Kujo, a rescue dog


*I don't have any idea what "see you soon"
means.*
-Joy, a Saluki Husky mix

*Bolting, digging, and eating poo are all signs of dog adolescence.*
-Da Vinci, Golden Lab

# Food and Water

*Dude I'm not begging; I'm just waiting.*
-Delta, a mixed breed

*If you limp when you get off the couch, you get a treat.*
-Prince, a Chihuahua


*Really the same thing for breakfast Again?*
-Spike, a Bull terrier


*If you stare at them where they eat dessert, they'll give you some.*
-Runner, a mixed breed

*I get a treat every time I run away and come back.*
-T-bone, a Bulldog Boxer mix

*If you ate this, you would fart too.*
-Peanuts, a inner-city street dog

*Peanut butter is like Xanax.*
-Ozzie, a Cocker Spaniel

*A garbage can is just a big dog bowl.*
-Bartholomew, a Mastiff

*If you don't get snacks at your house, ask for a toddler. Once you have a toddler, there's an endless supply of snacks.*
-Molly, a Golden Retriever

*If you bark at company, you get a treat to*
*stop.*
-Blueberry, a Chin Chihuahua mix


*If you stand and stare at your empty food*
*dish, they might give you a treat.*
-Buddy, a Black Lab


*My human doesn't understand the difference*
*between treats and teasing.*
-Van Gogh, a Doberman Pinscher

# Relationships

*I'll protect any child who shares his lunch with me.*
-Wags, a Golden Retriever

*Dogs understand yes and no but not share.*
-Rambo, a Terrier mix


*The 1st few years you have to interact with them. Then after that you can just lie around.*
-Blues, a Basset Hound


*Touching is my love language.*
-Nappy, a rescue dog

*Why will you scratch my ears but not my butt?*
-Nitro, a Pit Bull

*You said "walk", but you started playing tug-of-war.*
-Jughead, a Bullmastiff


*You have a strange way to check people out. Why not just sniff their butt?*
-Noah, a mixed breed


*Five years and you still don't know what I mean when I bark.*
-Texas, A Collie

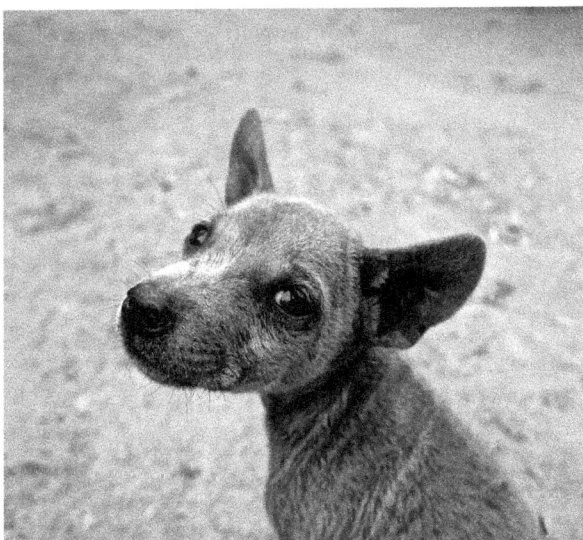

*I'm not sure if this Pen is a retreat or a prison cell.*
-Tag, a Chihuahua

*Babies look and sound like squeaky toys but they're not.*
-Autumn, a Black Lab


*We have to bump and run into you. We don't have arms to hug with.*
-Cutie, a Labradoodle

# Questions

***I found a dead bird in the yard; can we keep it?***
-Desoto, a Yorkshire Terrier

*You poop in the house, why can't I?*
-Justice, a German Shorthaired Pointer


*Whenever the doorbell rings you jump up and run around excited; why can't I?*
-Quincy, a Pug


(at the vets)
*You gonna cut what off?*
-Sarge, a Jack Russell Terrier

*You take natural supplements; why can't I eat rabbit poo?*
-Zulu, a Boxer Bulldog mix

*Can I have a bath so that I can go out and roll in the mud?*
-Sasha, a Beagle

*Why are you panting like that? You can sweat.*
-Tennessee, a Dachshund

*How am I supposed to know what Thunder is?*
-Patton, a Brittany

*How was I to know how much that cost?*
-Indigo, a Staffordshire Bull Terrier

*I can't see through doors. How do I know if it's the mailman or a clown?*
-Midget, a Weimaraner

*If God wanted us just to be petted behind our ears, why did he give us a belly?*
-Adam, a Lab Dalmatian mix

*You stare at the TV. Why can't I stare out the window?*
-Opal, a Pembroke

*If you're not trying to control me, why do I have to wear this collar?*
-Chaos, a Boston Terrier

*Why do you keep saying, "you can't do that"*
*when obviously I'm showing you that I can?*
-Crayon, an inner-city rescue dog

# Body Parts

***My butt itches.***
-Blossom, a Golden Retriever

*I wish you had a tail to cover your butt crack.*
-Buzz, a Shih Tzu


*Hair is like clothes, I change every day.*
-Hercules, a Havanese


*What do you scratch when your butt itches?*
-Puck, a mixed breed

*Touching you with either end is a sign of affection.*
-Liberty, a Lab

*Humans seem to be attracted the holes in your body.*
-Wilson, a French Bulldog

# Behavior

*They must say it over 3 times to really mean it.*
-Gizmo, a Poodle Schnauzer mix

*I don't have underwear, so I have to leave my hair on the floor.*
-Howler, a Husky


*Hey, do I say you're a "bad boy" when you chew on things when you're nervous?*
-Boots, a Boxer


*When was the last time you told someone you had to pee and they said to just hold it?*
-Ben, a Dachshund

*There is a reason we start out as puppies.*
-Cassie, a Pug

*Does "stop it" mean something different for me than for your kids?*
-Eggo, a Terrier mix

*If I love it, I Lick it.*
-Kipling, a Doberman Pinscher

*Of course, I'm scratching the door, it's how I knock.*
-Nova, a Poodle mix

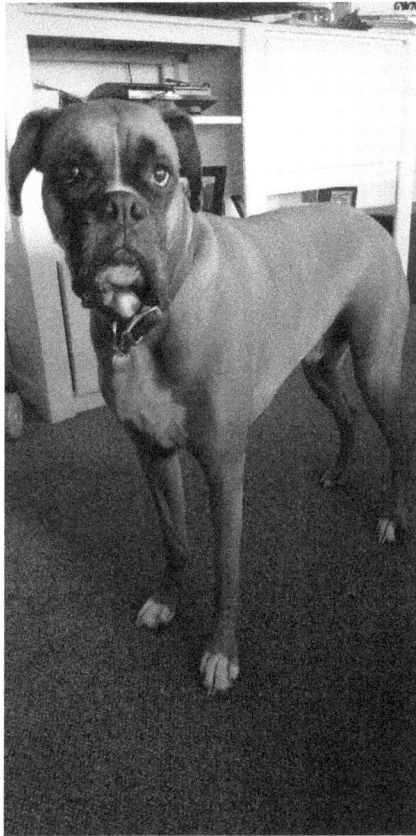

*You mean the back yard isn't an escape room?*
-Snoopy, a Pit Bull

*A leash is a tool they use to drag you or you use to drag them.*
-Orion, a Mastiff

*That siren doesn't scare me it just annoys me.*
-Pickles, a Terrier mix

*Remote controls do to look like chew toys.*
-Wookie, a Spaniel mix

***This is my house and I'll greet you any way I want to.***
-Repo, a Chihuahua

*I run around at the dog park because someone's chasing me.*
-Turbo, a Yorkshire Terrier


*One dog is for companionship. Two dogs are for competition. Three dogs are for Mayhem.*
-Durango, a mixed breed


*Most of us dogs only have a 2-speed transmission All or Nothing.*
-Emma, a German Shorthair Pointer

*Just because they can't do it they think it's silly.*
-Hoagie, a Maltese

## Poop and Pee

*Hey, you need to go outside and pick up a few things.*
-Fonzi, a Lab

*Do you pee in the shower? Is that why you expect me to pee in the rain?*
-Uma, mixed breed


*I'm not the only one that pees when I'm nervous.*
-April, a Brittany Spaniel


*Can you go 8 hours without peeing?*
-Bear, a Jack Russell Terrier

***I can't potty train myself.***
-Vanilla, a rescue dog

*Toilet paper is too tempting to eat.*
-Oreo, a Poodle


*You get up to go pee in the middle of the night.*
-Shadow, a mixed breed


*Sniffing poop is like smelling a shirt to see if it's clean.*
-Rocky, a pug

***Rabbit droppings are all natural.***
-Woodstock, a Rottweiler Husky mix

(at the vets)
*This place always smells like a ton of cats and dogs running around a pine forest.*
-Piper, a Pomeranian

Other Books by Redneck Mystic Media

*Available on Amazon*

Formation Football

Jesus and Baseball

Growing in Gratitude

www.ingramcontent.com/pod-product-compliance
Lightning Source LLC
Chambersburg PA
CBHW071735020426
42331CB00008B/2047